W9-BYA-104

The Path to Success Is Paved with

Positive Thinking

Blue Mountain Arts®

New and Best-Selling Titles

By Susan Polis Schutz:
To My Daughter with Love on the Important Things in Life
To My Son with Love

By Douglas Pagels:
For You, My Soul Mate
100 Things to Always Remember... and One Thing to Never Forget
Required Reading for All Teenagers

By Marci:
Friends Are Forever
10 Simple Things to Remember
To My Daughter
You Are My "Once in a Lifetime"

By Wally Amos, with Stu Glauberman:
The Path to Success Is Paved with Positive Thinking

By M. Butler and D. Mastromarino:
Take Time for You

By James Downton, Jr.:
Today, I Will... Words to Inspire Positive Life Changes

By Donna Fargo:
I Thanked God for You Today

Anthologies:
A Daughter Is Life's Greatest Gift
A Sister's Love Is Forever
A Son Is Life's Greatest Gift
Dream Big, Stay Positive, and Believe in Yourself
Friends for Life
God Is Always Watching Over You
Hang In There
Keep Believing in Yourself and Your Dreams
The Love Between a Mother and Daughter Is Forever
The Strength of Women
Think Positive Thoughts Every Day
Words Every Woman Should Remember

The Path to Success Is Paved with

Positive
Thinking

How to Live
a Joy-Filled Life
and Make Your
Dreams Come True

Wally Amos
with Stu Glauberman

Blue Mountain Press™
Boulder, Colorado

The publishers gratefully acknowledge the permission granted by Harcourt, Inc., for "I tell you the past is a bucket of ashes," from "Prairie" from THE COMPLETE POEMS OF CARL SANDBURG. Copyright © 1970, 1969 by Lillian Sandburg, Trustee. Reprinted by permission. All rights reserved.

Library of Congress Catalog Card Number: 2007042389
ISBN: 978-1-59842-257-3

▉ and Blue Mountain Press are registered in U.S. Patent and Trademark Office. Certain trademarks are used under license.

Printed in China.
Eighth Printing: 2013

♻ This book is printed on recycled paper.

This book is printed on archival quality, white felt, 110 lb. paper. This paper has been specially produced to be acid free (neutral pH) and contains no groundwood or unbleached pulp. It conforms with all the requirements of the American National Standards Institute, Inc., so as to ensure that this book will last and be enjoyed by future generations.

Library of Congress Cataloging-in-Publication Data

Amos, Wally.
    The path to success is paved with positive thinking : how to live a joy-filled life and make your dreams come true / Wally Amos with Stu Glauberman.
        p. cm.
    ISBN 978-1-59842-257-3 (trade pbk. : alk. paper) 1. Success. 2. Conduct of life. 3. Expectation (Psychology) 4. Persistence. 5. Perseverance (Ethics) I. Glauberman, Stu. II. Title.

    BF637.S8A485 2008
    650.1--dc22

                                                                    2007042389

Blue Mountain Arts, Inc.
P.O. Box 4549, Boulder, Colorado 80306

Contents

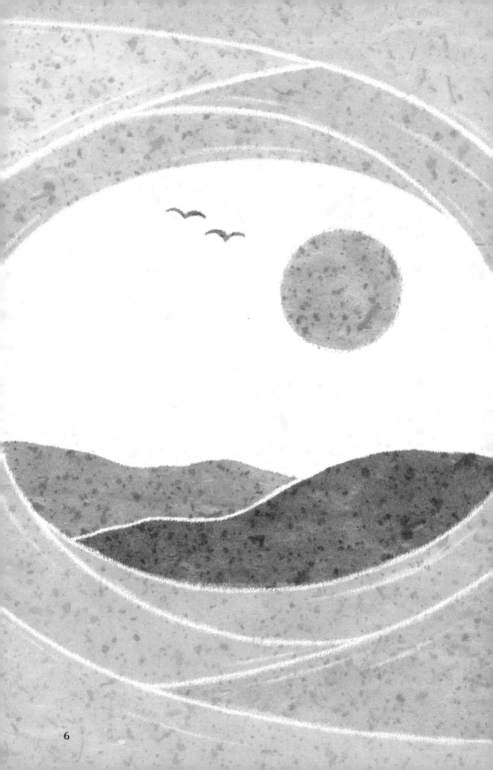

Positive Thinking
Will Take You Anywhere You Want to Go

A positive attitude is one of the secret
ingredients you need to discover and fulfill
your life's dreams. It is not the cure-all for
everything that ails you or a magic potion for
making you the smartest student in class or the
most successful person on the planet — but
coupled with other good qualities it will help
you flourish and become the best you can be.
High self-esteem, commitment, integrity, the
gift of giving, imagination, enthusiasm, faith,
and that old standby, love, are some of the
other ingredients.

Your attitude toward the world hinges on how
you look at yourself. As you lift yourself up,
you'll find that the world outside becomes a
reflection of what you are within.

Always remember... you'll get a lot farther on
one gallon of optimistic thinking than you will
on a tankful of negative thoughts. The power
in you begins with a positive attitude. So let's
get started!

The Keys to an Optimistic Outlook

Here's a dozen — make it a (cookie) baker's dozen — tips on how to discover and fulfill your dreams:

1. Stop being your own worst enemy. Be your own best friend.

2. Don't put yourself down. Pull yourself up.

3. Don't permit others to define who you are. You cannot be a failure without your own consent.

4. Respect yourself. Place a high value on yourself.

5. Take stock of who you are and what you're capable of. Work on weaknesses and find new strengths every day.

6. Replace "I can't" with "I can" and "I will."

7. Treat yourself generously, the way you want others to treat you.

8. Be compassionate. Love yourself and others will love you.

9. Remember that you are an individual expression of God. As a work of God's art, you are priceless and irreplaceable.

10. Visualize what you want from life, then work toward it. See it, then be it.

11. Allow time to be by yourself, with yourself. Take time to appreciate yourself.

12. Enjoy your uniqueness. Out of all the billions of people since the beginning of time, there has never been, and never will be, another you.

13. Realize that you are important to the entire world; what happens to the world begins with you.

Change your *thoughts* and you will literally **transform** *your life* and the **world**.

Imagine the Possibilities

One of the greatest truths I've discovered is that my thoughts create my reality. That's a really great reason to be positive.

Things happen in your life because of the thoughts you project. To change what happens to you, you must change your thoughts. Not only are you your own human projector, you are the star, writer, producer, director, and editor of your personal real-life documentary. For me, discovering that my thoughts produce the events in my life is right up there with the discovery of fire. It's real freedom!

You've heard it said many ways: "Thoughts are things," "As a man thinketh, so is he," "Like attracts like," and so on. You can hear it a thousand times, but it won't work until you begin to work it.

Make a commitment to yourself and begin to be positive!

Be Persistent

A word I learned early on was "stick-to-itiveness." It means unwavering tenacity, perseverance. Stick-to-itiveness has taught me that if I keep on keeping on, I will succeed.

Perseverance is more than maintaining. It is also preparing. Preparing while you persevere will create a steady pace toward achieving your goals and increase your faith during those rough and threatening times. It will help you cultivate patience, planning, and timing. The reward for stick-to-itiveness is the satisfaction of knowing you stayed the course and got the desired results.

Are you truly committed? Do you make statements like "I guess," "I hope," or "I'll try"? If you do, then you are not committed. Commitment is "I will!" When you say "I will," energy goes out to attract whatever or whomever you need to help you achieve your goal.

Stay Committed

How does one gather the strength and courage to keep on keeping on?

1. Be honest with yourself. Many of us do not honestly evaluate our situations. We don't want to believe it's as bad as it is, and we keep pouring good money and time into a bad situation.

2. Own your own mistakes. Being a victim is not healthy or productive. The quicker you identify and own your mistakes, the quicker you move ahead.

3. Focus on answers and solutions. Do not become part of the problem by living in it and constantly reviewing how bad it is. The problem doesn't change until you solve it. Stay out of yesterday, wait for tomorrow, and live in the present.

4. Have faith! Your human capabilities are limited. The answers come through you, not from you. Do your best, then let your higher power take over.

Remember, things are never as bad as they seem.

Everyone who has achieved greatness or fulfillment in life started out with a **dream**... An unlimited power to create lies within **you**.

It All Starts
with a Dream...

The universe has an immeasurable number of ideas running through it. When you tune into the wonder of creation — if you have faith and allow the higher source to work through you — you become a finely tuned channel for ideas to flow consistently through you. If you do not hear the ideas, that does not mean they are not there. It means your spirit is tuned into some other frequency. Intuition and instinct will tell you when to take action and what to do.

We create opportunities for ourselves... Seize each moment and make intelligent and honest use of it. Some attempts will pay off, and eventually at least one will hit the jackpot! If you stay in the game, making adjustments now and then, and keep swinging the bat, sooner or later you'll hit the ball. Live your life to the fullest, because the goodwill and energy you project attract opportunity to you in proportion to your effort.

Plan for Tomorrow, but Live in Today

Oftentimes we review events in our lives
wishing the outcome had been different.
Carl Sandburg displayed great wisdom
when he wrote, "I tell you the past
    is a bucket of ashes."
Yesterday is a word, not a place
you can return to.
Living in the past prevents you
from taking advantage
of the many opportunities present
    in today.

There have been many events in my life
that I wish would have had
    a different outcome.
Neither wishing nor anything else
can change events of the past.

I've had to face each situation head-on,
accept it, look for the answers
    and solutions,
and move on with my life.
Whether you're dealing with
a personal or business challenge,
you need to make an accurate
assessment of the situation,
accept the fact that it has occurred,
review your options,
create a plan of action,
and get on with your life.

Equally as destructive as living
    in the past
is worrying about the future.
There is no such place as the future.
It's just a word, not a place you can visit...
Accept the realities of today.
Plan for tomorrow,
but live in today.

The antidote to worry is *action*. **Do** something! As you begin to *focus* on doing, you will get results and a new perspective on your situation.

Take Action

No matter how large or small the problem, it's important not to take on the whole thing. Break it down into smaller, more manageable pieces. Do not become anxious, worried, or frustrated.

Most problems are combinations of puzzles, obstacles, and entanglements. It is easier for you to focus on answers and solutions when you break the problems down into their more basic elements. We've all heard the sayings "By the inch it's a cinch, by the yard it's hard," and "How do you eat an elephant? One bite at a time." They're both true. We can handle anything in small increments.

See your problems as friends to help you expand your critical thinking capability. Also remember they did not come to stay; they came to pass.

Attitude Is the Magic Word

Just as what you believe creates your reality, how you believe determines your degree of success. That *how* is your attitude. A consistently positive, energetic attitude is one of the main ingredients to help you create a positive reality.

We already know that what we believe creates our reality — so believe in a positive attitude! That means taking over what you can control in your life. You can't control someone else's attitude, but you can control how you react to that person.

The best way to develop a positive attitude is by watching the words you use. I talk about the concept of "plus" words — ones that encourage — and "minus" words that can destroy. In order to succeed we need to understand that words, whether spoken to yourself or by others, are powerful and can make or break you or another person. The following story is a strong case for giving positive support:

A group of frogs was traveling through the woods and two of them fell into a deep pit. All the other frogs gathered around the pit. When they saw how deep the pit was, they told the unfortunate frogs they would never get out. The two frogs ignored the comments and tried to jump up out of the pit.

The other frogs kept telling them to stop, that they were as good as dead. Finally, one of the frogs took heed to what the other frogs were saying and simply gave up. He fell down and died.

The other frog continued to jump as hard as he could. Once again, the crowd of frogs yelled at him to stop the pain and suffering and just die. He jumped even harder and finally made it out. When he got out, the other frogs asked him, "Why did you continue jumping? Didn't you hear us?"

The frog explained to them that he was deaf. He thought they were encouraging him the entire time.

There is a power of life and death in our words. Develop a positive attitude by speaking "plus" words.

Create *your own*

belief system and feel

the **power** *of the words*
"I can" and "I will."

You Can Do It!

There's no sense in
wallowing in the negative
when you could be doing
something positive
to improve your life.

A sure cure for low self-esteem
is to achieve something
on your own.
With your accomplishment,
you prove something to yourself
   and the universe.
You show the world
that you can do what you
set out to do.
It's like playing pinball
or computer games:
every time you get past an obstacle
and solve a problem for yourself,
you chalk up personal points
toward higher self-esteem.
So score one for you.
Decide you are a "can-do" person,
and you will become a "will-do" person.

Your Words Create Your Reality

Words are powerful tools.
Yet unless we use them carefully
and communicate clearly,
they are of little value.
Many of our difficulties
in human relations
are caused by improper
or inadequate communication.
When communication is not clear,
one of two things occurs.
Either we do not get our ideas
across to other people,
or we do not hear
what others are saying to us.
Misunderstandings usually result.

Relationships may be filled
with gaps of silence that beg
for compliments, consolations,
words of encouragement,
or a simple "I love you."

We underestimate how powerful
our words and thoughts are —
not only to the person
they are directed to,
but also to ourselves.
Just as words spoken carelessly
can cause pain and misunderstanding,
words not spoken
at the appropriate time
can be equally harmful.
You project your energy
through everything you say and do.
If you're not careful,
negative thoughts will slip out —
and nothing good ever comes from that.

Give more importance
to your words.
Realize their tremendous power
and use only those words
that support, encourage,
and are truthful, happy, and joyful.
Use positive words...
and watch your power soar.

Your *dreams*
and *goals*

become a reality

to the extent that you

pour *yourself*

into them.

Anything Is Possible

There are no promises that life will be easy. However, easy or hard is not the question. I'm convinced the only question we need ever ask is: "Is this possible?" The answer will always be yes because all things are possible, especially when we apply faith — if only the size of a mustard seed — and a lot of patience.

If you give yourself wholeheartedly to each assignment, you can reach astonishing heights. Each task offers you something to learn which you might draw on one day. Every new thing you learn provides you with an opportunity to improve yourself in the future.

You will receive abundant rewards for going out of your way to give more than is required of you. If you habitually invest only minimum amounts of energy into your obligations, you end up with a life that is minimally happy. One of the best ways to advance your life is to go that extra mile.

Have Faith in Your Abilities

You can always turn lemons
    into lemonade.
Remember that doors may slam
    in your face,
yet others will always open
to more brilliant prospects.
See any adverse situation
you may currently have
as the necessary impetus
for creating a fabulous future...
This acceptance will recharge you
and become a powerful force
    in your renewal.
Don't allow yourself
to see any event as a defeat.
Don't give up or complain
about what has happened
or give in to the ridiculous notion
that you are a failure.
Instead, throw aside all the negative beliefs
and begin to explore the possibilities ahead.

Five Promises
You Can Make to Yourself

1. To listen more — to the people around you and also to your inner voice. On any given day, someone you know can have an idea that will change your life.

2. To be more patient and less impulsive — to think things through before taking action. No decision is so important that it can't wait for you to review it. You may realize it has to be done ASAP, a little later, or not at all.

3. To constantly evaluate your performance — and see how you can improve on a daily basis.

4. To not push so hard — realizing that not everything depends solely on you.

5. To remember that life is a team effort — and you are part of the team. You can also keep in mind that there is a power greater than the whole team, and allow that power an opportunity to perform.

Once you begin to **believe** in yourself, others will begin to believe in *you*. Once you place a high value on yourself, others will **value** you as well.

Harness the Power of Self-Esteem

To hold something in esteem means to hold it in favorable regard, to consider it valuable. Self-esteem is to hold yourself in high regard, to think of yourself as a hot property, a uniquely valuable individual, a one-of-a-kind collector's item.

Many people blame their low self-esteem and feelings of inferiority on others. But you cannot have low self-esteem thrust upon you without your permission. You can't be stepped on again and again unless you lie down and let people step all over you. You always have the choice: pick yourself up off the floor, get up and go forward, or lie there and play dead. If you choose to move ahead, you are emancipated; from that point on, you are 100 percent responsible for your self-image.

To harness the power of self-esteem and make it work for you, begin by acknowledging that you have the free will and free choice to take full responsibility for who you are, how you see yourself, and what direction you're going to point yourself in. There's only one person who can lift your low self-esteem and raise it up to the heights of self-love and self-confidence, and that's you.

Live According to Your Highest Ideals

Dedication to high ideals is like a trademark. It becomes an identity that you can wear with great pride.

Let your mind learn and search and believe in the perfectibility of things — because if you allow it, it will create beauty. By seeking to understand and improve upon your world, you will come to live happily and substantially on the journey to greatness and happiness.

If you want the very best for yourself, your family, society, and this world... be prepared to live in an honorable fashion with every action you take. Give the best of yourself, and you will get the best in return.

Believe in Your Own Greatness

Everyone on this earth has the power to tap into their own greatness and the laws of the universe to find joy and fulfillment.

If you believe you will win, the odds immediately become stacked in your favor.

Success doesn't come to you; you go to it. With a winning attitude, anything is possible.

There is always a way
to make *victory* out of
adversity, so long as you
keep focused on *answers*
and *solutions*.

Don't Let Problems Hold You Back

The main thought that helps me bounce back is to know that if I roll over, I am sure to lose. You see, the only way you fail is to give up. If you keep on keeping on, you will find the answer you seek or a better answer.

I am also helped by realizing that each experience holds a lesson for me and is an opportunity for me to grow. Seeing life from this vantage point helps you to own each experience and relive more intelligently those you have to repeat. A positive mental attitude enables you to seek solutions and answers instead of playing the victim.

Crises can turn out to be glorious benefits if we draw on universal wisdom to handle them. Challenges are more than simply part of every human being's journey; they are valuable catalysts for our personal growth.

Know How to Overcome Any Crisis

1. Don't become part of the problem. When you are faced with an unpleasant situation, do not internalize the dispute or defend yourself in a combative manner. Concentrate on the worthwhile things in your life.

2. Accept and acknowledge the reality of your situation. You have to say to yourself, "This is the way it is, and the course of events now depends entirely on me." You can only deal with your problem once you separate your emotions from the facts. Once you do that, you gain control of your situation and can make the moves necessary to resolve it.

3. Remain committed. Even when you privately may think things could not be worse, you should still wake up each morning determined to stay the course. Keep your heart and mind completely on track, and never give up.

4. Allow the experience to open you up to what you need to learn. Every situation is an education. If you open your mind to the voices of others, you will open your life and enhance your chances for growth and achievement.

5. Maintain a positive mental attitude. Regardless of the appearance of a situation, there is always good to be found. Make sure you seek out the beauty and wisdom in everything. Believe it or not, it is always there to be found.

6. Hold on to your faith. When you have faith, you reinforce your subconscious to make your life move forward and flourish. You create your own circumstances; your subconscious merely reproduces in your environment what you conjure up in your mind.

7. Consciously practice living in the present. It always helps to be mindful and aware of each moment so that you can make best use of the time you have. If you waste your energy on thinking about what can go wrong, you inhibit your ability to live each day effectively. If you live in the moment, you realize that you have everything you need to deal with your life. The past cannot be changed nor the future predicted, but each moment in the present is a building block to a happy existence.

To get where

you want to go,

it's important to understand

where you've been. But don't let

what happened yesterday

affect your **positive** outlook

today or your hopes for

the **future**.

Leave the Past Behind

Are you living in the past today? Are you letting past negative experiences influence the choices you make in your daily life?

Many people have trouble separating what they have done and what has happened to them from who they are. They think they are their behavior. However, you are not your behavior. You are separate from and more than your behavior. You are not your parents' divorce. You are not a lost job, a lost love, or a lost opportunity.

When you begin to appreciate the fantastic being that you are, you will also begin to see a change in your behavior. Coming to terms with your past helps you to love yourself, which changes how you relate to others in your world. Learn to look at the past as a notebook or template that needs to be opened up and written upon. It's up to each of us to take our past and improve upon it.

What to Do When You Hit Bottom

Do you remember what it is like to be a kid sliding down a water slide? Frightened or not, you knew instinctively that you were going to hit bottom. And even the smallest child knows that when you reach the bottom, you've got to stand up.

If you lose touch with the power that's in you, it's easy to slide into the abyss of despair. But if you think hard and look closely, you'll find there's always a lifeline to latch on to and pull yourself up with.

Sometimes when you start thinking things aren't going your way, you count all the "bad things" that are happening and total them up with the certainty that nothing good will happen. It's like pushing yourself down a hill or kicking yourself when you're already down.

There are times when we can all relate to the title of songwriter and poet Richard Fariña's 1960s novel *Been Down So Long It Looks like Up to Me*. There are many excuses for being down, but if you take a positive attitude, things can only look up.

How long should you allow yourself to stay down? Don't wait for the ten count. Don't wait a minute longer than it takes to stand up.

In his hit song, "Limbo Rock," when Chubby Checker asked, "How low can you go?" he wasn't challenging people to go from bad to worse. He was encouraging them to bend their backs and emerge triumphantly limber from under the limbo pole. Sometimes it may seem you'll never be able to bend and come out from under the barriers that are getting you down. The only way to overcome obstacles is to continue working your way through them.

No one ever issued an insurance policy to guarantee that life would be easy. When everything seems to be at its gloomiest, remember that the darkest hour is just before the dawn. Seen another way, the darkest hour is precisely the time for you to shine, because it's in the darkest sky that you get the best view of the stars. After that, you can enjoy the quiet beauty of dawn and the start of a bright new day.

The **means**

create the ends —

and the ends will be

great

if the means is *love*.

Everything Works Out for the Best

Everything works out to enhance your life — even if it appears to be distinctly the opposite! All you need to do is trust in this natural law as an unfailing truth and have faith that change can never threaten who you deeply and truly are inside.

You can come through the worst hardships and triumph over your troubles. You will find in every apparent disaster the seeds of new choices and an incredible future.

I have been shown innumerable times that my faith in a supreme truth is completely well-founded. But I've also had to take committed action to get there, learning from experience along the way. My faith in the eventual outcome provides me with the confidence to accept each chapter in my life story as vital to my growth and my journey toward the goal, no matter how difficult that episode may be.

Keep Moving Toward Your Goals

Confucius said, "It does not matter how slowly you go, so long as you do not stop." Truer words were never spoken. You succeed by not stopping. I notice it when I take my morning walk. I take the first step and keep going until I reach my destination or my desired time limit.

The question you need to ask yourself is, "If this principle works in routine, everyday occurrences, why wouldn't it work in all areas of my life?" Of course, the answer is that it does. I'll bet if you reviewed your successes in your own life, you would find this principle at work. You don't have to be extra smart. It does not matter what sex, race, or color you happen to be. What counts is not quitting.

You are guaranteed to lose if you quit. You never know what will happen if you just keep going. So go as slow or as fast as you need to go. But whatever you do, please do not stop.

Don't Let Everyday Distractions Sidetrack You

How do you keep from getting sidetracked by the daily distractions in life? Create a reminder that helps you stay focused and positive.

Write on a sheet of paper, "I can be five times more enthusiastic about life!" Underline "five times" five times. Rip the paper in half and ball the two pieces into a tiny wad. Tie a rubber band around the wad to keep it together. It's been twelve years since I first did this exercise in a classroom in Charlotte, NC. I've gone through a few wads of paper because when I lose or give one away, I immediately create another. I feel lost if I do not have it in my pocket. Not only does it remind me to be more enthusiastic, but also more loving, more giving, and more faith-filled. It's a constant reminder that I can always increase the positive characteristics of life times five, times five, etc. Why not create your own credo using something personal and special to you? Review it frequently. Share it with others. If it inspires and motivates you, it will do the same for them. This might just be the answer to help you stay positive.

If you can find at least
one *positive* outcome in
each instance of adversity and
focus on the positive,
before long, from the bitterness
will come
sweetness.

You Can Always Profit from Your Mistakes

The Irish writer Oscar Wilde once quipped, "Experience is simply the name we give our mistakes." We all make mistakes, but a bigger mistake is harping on them until they drive us wild. A singer will record the same song many times. Each recording is called a take. Let's say that after the 99th recording, the producer asks everyone to listen to take 99. Everyone listens with one goal in mind: how to improve take 99. No one condemns it or judges it. After everyone gives his or her input, the producer says, "All right everyone, places, we're rolling, take 100." Take 99 was not a failure; it was just a *mis-take*. Life is just a series of takes that we sometimes call experience. Inherent in each take (experience) is a lesson. Learn the lesson and move on.

Mistakes happen and misfortunes strike even the most cautious planners and the luckiest gamblers. But sometimes the harder you fall, the stronger you become. It's called process. You can't change your past, but you can accept it and maybe even profit from it. The faster you process your unfortunate experiences and identify your positive outcomes, the faster your life will become a happy one.

Overcome Negative Thoughts

Positive thinking can overcome fear, anguish, anxiety, and despair. The Buddhist teacher Thich Nhat Hanh explains that mindfulness, or being conscious of your thoughts and actions, can overcome negative thoughts about yourself that have become habitual. "Our joy, our peace, our happiness depend very much on our practice of recognizing and transforming our habit energies," he says.

When negative thoughts come to mind, you should recognize them and, in this way, take control of the situation. Don't fight the negativity to the point where you hate yourself more; just alert yourself to it and work on the negativity until you can wrap it with a positive energy that springs up naturally.

Acceptance Is the Key to Changing Yourself

Acceptance is a powerful tool in building a positive attitude. Once you have acceptance, you can begin to change what you don't like about yourself. Being able to laugh at yourself is another step toward positive self-esteem. If you can see the humor in something you've done, you can forgive yourself, shake it off, and move on. Laughter is good both for your soul and your attitude.

Say you've evolved to the point where you accept most everything about your body and only dislike one part that's either too small or too big or too straight or too crooked. You could spend thousands of dollars on plastic surgery and risk your good health for the rest of your life, or you could *get over it and accept it!*

The Nobel Peace Prize-winning activist Nelson Mandela, who helped defeat the apartheid system that had kept his fellow South Africans in submission for a century, said: "It is what we make out of what we have, not what we are given, that separates one person from another." Expect the treatment you deserve for being the fully evolved human being you really are.

Change is like

shedding one's skin —

it allows a

more **beautiful** *you*

to emerge.

You Are Constantly Evolving

Conventional education does not teach us the truth that change is a positive force in our lives, and that it can act as a voyage of discovery from which great benefit may come.

Challenging situations are opportunities for growth and progress. Resolve to be easy on yourself and approach the future with a positive attitude. Come to terms with the fact that change is the one constant in life, and every turn of events has a purpose. You cannot see into the future, but you can reach a point of peace where you rejoice in the opportunity to move on to new challenges and opportunities.

Every seeming problem in your world has the potential to propel you to your wildest dreams if you are no longer confined by the expectation of limitations. Believe that the power within you will produce success; trust in the perfection of the people and experiences that come across your path.

Lead by Example

By being a leader, you can inspire those around you to have a more positive outlook in their own lives. There are many qualities you may need to become an effective leader. Here are some of them...

1. Be humble. The brash, abrasive leader will have a hard time getting the cooperation of others.

2. Be willing to admit you are wrong. Admitting your mistakes and being vulnerable will inspire those around you to give more of themselves.

3. Encourage those around you to express their creativity by performing tasks using *their* ideas, rather than *you* telling or showing them *your* way. Life is trial and error; we learn by doing. People who feel free to find their own way and take risks will feel better about themselves and what they're doing.

4. Pretend you're having fun and enjoying what you're doing even if you're not. If people around you see you enjoying yourself, they'll enjoy themselves.

Remember, we lead by example.

Be a Team Player

In order to be successful in any area of life, it is necessary to be part of a team. "Team" stands for "Together Everyone Achieves More." The only thing we can do alone is fail.

Whether you're part of a team in sports, in a one-on-one relationship, in business, or in the volunteer sector, you stand to benefit greatly by being a positive, unselfish contributor for the good of the team. I love the quote: "I am more than I am, but less than we are."

My attitude says that I am a member of the greater community, planet Earth, and when I give to the community, I give to myself. We're all members of the same team, the human race. Let's make a commitment today to serve one another.

What a

world this would be

if every human being

recognized the **value**

of every other human being

and helped to pull others **up**

instead of down!

Shine a Positive Light on Everyone You Meet

His Holiness the 14th Dalai Lama of Tibet, the spiritual and temporal leader of Tibetan Buddhists, began a talk on self-reliance with these words: "Within all beings there is a seed of perfection. However compassion is needed in order to activate that seed, which is inherent in our hearts and minds." In *The Art of Happiness*, the Dalai Lama suggests that the way to avoid loneliness and isolation is to look for positive attributes in everyone you meet and approach them in a positive way, with compassion in your mind. In this manner, all the positives will add up: yours, theirs, and the positive nature of the universe.

Self-esteem and love are intertwined. You've got to love yourself before you can love anyone. If you think of yourself as an individual expression of God or a priceless work of God's art, you'll find it easy to love yourself and pass that love on to others.

Don't Be Overly Influenced by Others

In life, we have a tendency sometimes to be overly concerned with what others are doing. There is a children's song that actually gives some great advice about this...

Row, row, row your boat... You can't win by being concerned about how fast or slow the other boats are going. The smallest distraction can break your stride and cause you to lose the race. Your job is to prepare, concentrate, and practice rowing your own boat.

Gently down the stream... Not angrily or boisterously, but calmly, gently. Keep a level head and go with the current. When you get upset, you lose focus and your thinking becomes unclear. Being gentle and patient creates positive results.

Merrily, merrily, life is but a dream... Projects seem to progress more effortlessly when you're having fun. Enjoying what you do takes the sting out of it. Tell yourself, "I'm not serious but I'm responsible." You can be responsible and still have fun. Lighten up and enjoy the ride.

Express Yourself

Never let the negative opinions of others place a value on who you are and what you're worth. Who cares what others think of you or what you're doing? You certainly shouldn't. And it's okay to make mistakes even if others choose to scoff. There is no one on earth who hasn't made a misstep and fallen on his or her face.

One of the most important lessons in life is that you count and what you think counts. It takes everyone and everything and every idea to make the universe whole.

Unfortunately, it takes some people a lifetime before they realize it's okay to speak their minds. Many people spend their whole lives waiting for wisdom and experience and only find their voices to say what they really think when they have already lost their teeth. I agree with Oprah Winfrey, who has done more for raising self-esteem than anyone else on television. She advises that it's more important to say what you believe than it is to hold your tongue to keep the peace or please others.

Learning to express what you think is another step toward building your self-confidence and being all that you can be.

Love the

inner you and

keep moving *ahead*,

because you can't

stand still and

improve at the

same time.

Be Sure to Love Yourself

Develop love for yourself. Stop condemning yourself and learn to love you as you are, even though you might not like some of your physical features or character traits... If you're not satisfied with certain attributes, develop a program to change them. If you do something you know isn't in your best interest or not at your highest level of thinking, acknowledge that you have done it, forgive yourself, and move on.

Don't be too hard on yourself. Know you're going to make mistakes, and realize you'll grow through them. If you didn't make mistakes, you'd stay at the same level of achievement and your life would be very boring. Besides, there are really no such things as mistakes — just learning experiences.

It would help us all to remember the times we made mistakes and to realize we are all in training and in a state of becoming a better parent, student, friend, or employee.

You're More Than What You Own

Some people imagine themselves to be lacking because they don't have the designer clothes, the big house with a picket fence, or the sports car or private jet they were conditioned to want. Wanting material things is the high-octane fuel that keeps the fires of self-esteem burning low. If you fancy that you need fancy things to give yourself value, you will probably never have enough things and never value yourself.

As children, we're conditioned to believe that good looks and money can bring happiness. But if money is all that matters to you, you'll never have enough and you won't be happy with any less. If you rely on material things to give meaning to your life, you'll be miserable when you see that someone else's stuff is even better and more expensive than your stuff.

The antidote to this addictive poison is to focus on the God-given things you were born with and the endless possibilities of what you can achieve. Thinking about your birth can do wonders to elevate your self-esteem and help you create a new and improved you.

There's No Better Gift Than This Moment

There's sweetness to be had in living in the moment. If you don't make up your mind to live life to the fullest now, you probably never will. If you're not having fun now because you're waiting, just waiting, for your dream to come true, you likely never will.

It's a certainty that tomorrow and every day will have twenty-four hours. What you choose to do with them is up to you. Why wait until you hit retirement age, or whatever age you have in mind, to enjoy life? Imagine how very sad it will be to look back and say, "I wish I'd done more when I was younger. I wish I'd taken more trips. I wish I'd pursued that hobby or pastime or played the kazoo more often when I was younger." Well, you're younger than that age now, so what's your excuse?

Having fun is a choice. Taking charge of your life is a choice. So why not choose now? Choose to start having fun today. Choose to make the most of every day. Choose to discover and fulfill your life dreams.

Quit making excuses.

Time is passing — act now

on your **deepest** desires.

Make a commitment, create a plan,

and let your **every** action from

this day forward lead you to doing

what you **love** to do.

It Really Is Up to You

When you take responsibility for your life and your actions, you cease being a victim. When you cease being a victim, you no longer look for anything or anyone to blame for your failures. As a matter of fact, when you cease being a victim, you no longer have failures. Your perception clears and events that do not work out as you had planned are seen as steppingstones or rungs in your ladder to success. Your time and energy are focused on solutions and answers. You clearly understand that "If it is to be, it is up to me."

Situations are not always to your liking. They don't always appear to be to your advantage, but you have to accept them. If it's in your power to change them, do whatever you can. If not, you must accept them as they are and move on with your life.

Don't Waste a
Single Moment on Anger

The great philosopher Ralph Waldo Emerson once said, "For every minute you are angry, you lose sixty seconds of happiness." Learning how to handle your anger effectively will go a long way toward building and maintaining a positive attitude.

So how do you deal with angry feelings? Are you controlling them — or do they control you? Do you find yourself yelling at your children, spouse, friends, or coworkers because they do not respond quickly enough or do things your way? Remember that once angry words leave your mouth, it's impossible to take them back.

As you go through your days, become conscious of any anger you may have and how it might damage others. Make a special effort to be more loving and considerate of the people in your life by using words of support and comfort instead of words that threaten and destroy. You'll feel a lot better about yourself — and those around you will, too.

Your Three Best Assets

A Positive Attitude. The glass is neither half full nor half empty; it's overflowing! The glass is a metaphor for life, and your thoughts and attitude determine its capacity. When you're positive and upbeat, good things can happen. When you're negative and depressed, things tend to go wrong. A positive attitude is a great gift.

Peace of Mind. Give up the need to control everyone and every situation in your life. There's a saying that applies here: "For peace of mind, give up being General Manager of the Universe." Give yourself the gift of peace of mind.

Love. You are special and unique. You deserve your love. In fact, life has no meaning unless you love yourself. Some people think it is selfish and egotistical to love yourself — but it's impossible to give another what you do not have yourself.

The great thing about these gifts is you don't have to fight the crowds at the mall and there are no out-of-pocket costs. They are nonreturnable and renewable. What a deal!

Kindness

is **contagious**.

Pass it on.

The Power of Giving

There is no greater satisfaction than assisting the world in a positive way. Through helping others, you not only earn the love and support of those who receive; the spirit of giving also spreads through the universe.

The most beneficial means for dealing with your issues is to devote time and energy often to the difficulties of others. Such action puts your own needs in context and diminishes the size of your troubles. At the same time, of course, your fellow human beings are helped!

Seek to make a positive contribution in thought, word, and deed. We all have much to give and much to gain by giving, because every time we favor others, our supply of good fortune is nourished. Just as one and one are two universally, so too is the principle of giving and receiving.

The Power of "Please" and "Thank You"

Please and *thank you* are three of the most powerful words in our vocabulary, as well as the most underutilized. As children, we are taught that these magic words will unlock any door and provide us with our most cherished wishes. How many times were you asked as a kid, "What's the magic word?" You knew it was *please*.

In today's fast-paced, high-tech world we have forgotten the basics. I don't mean reading, writing, and arithmetic; I mean the basics in manners. Saying *please* and *thank you* tells other people that you value and respect them. It says you do not view them as inanimate objects. You recognize their humanness.

In all situations, giving is receiving. As you lift the spirits and feelings of another, you feel better about yourself. Try being very clear and distinct when saying *please* and *thank you*; you'll immediately begin to notice how friendly and cooperative people are toward you. You'll also notice how good it makes you feel.

Adding *please* and *thank you* to your vocabulary will gain you the respect of others, plus increase your respect for yourself.

The Best Way to
Help Others

The motivation to nourish another
is never to receive nourishment
   in return.
It's really extending yourself
to acknowledge a fellow human being.
It is an act of kindness
deeply rooted in love —
a love for all humanity.
It says that you honor and respect
   all people.
Nourishing others also shows
that you bring understanding
into every situation.
It has the potential to bring
   peace to our planet.

The best way to change another person is to
change yourself. Your own behavior and attitude
are the only things completely under your control.

Life

is made **rich**

through our

relationships,

not through

money.

We Are All a Part of One Another

The first and most important relationship in your life is oftentimes overlooked. That's your relationship with yourself. If it's not positive then none of your other relationships will be. We spend more time with ourselves each day than we do with anyone else. We spend hours each day communicating with ourselves, either consciously or unconsciously.

The first step toward developing a positive relationship with yourself is to begin loving yourself unconditionally. Stop the negative self-talk. Be more gentle with and accepting of yourself. The results will benefit you for a lifetime.

It does not matter what your career is or what business you're in; the strength of your relationships will determine the level of your success. You can live without a brother or a sister, but you cannot live without a friend. We are always in relationships. Keep them positive by nourishing them.

Let the Sun Shine In

Are you the kind of person who lets rainy days and Mondays get you down? Psychologists say that prolonged bad weather can lead to depression and dampen your enthusiasm, leaving you feeling blue. They call this condition Seasonal Affective Disorder, or SAD for short.

I'm no psychologist, but it occurs to me that both the disorder and the cure are in the mind. If the sky is black and the rain won't stop, grab a philosophical umbrella and let the sun figuratively shine in. You can shop if you like to shop, spend time with friends who are fun to be with, or curl up with a good book. Whatever you do, if you do it with a sunny attitude inside, you can beat the weather outside. You'll suffer from JOY instead of SAD. Joy comes from within.

Take Time to Be Happy

Enthusiasm creates joy. Joy creates more joy. Maintaining a joyful outlook and keeping a high level of enthusiasm can sometimes be difficult, but the more you do it, the easier it gets. The rewards always reflect what you invest.

Two ingredients are necessary for success in life — fun and fearlessness. I am suggesting you replace fear with faith and look for the fun in everyday experiences.

How many times a day do you laugh? If you don't have at least four or five belly laughs a day, you're missing out on a very important ingredient in life: fun. It's the one thing in life that can get you through any situation stress free.

When we give up

forcing a situation to conform

to how *we* think it *should* be

and allow it to be the way it's

supposed to be, life becomes

a whole lot *easier.*

Life *works* if you let it.

Be patient! Be positive.

Every Experience Holds a Vital Lesson

I'd like to suggest we stop "going through" our life experiences and start "growing through" them. Every experience holds a vital lesson. If we continue being victims, complaining about how bad things are, we fail to see the lesson. However, if we enter the experience knowing it might be somewhat painful for a while but will eventually get better, then we can begin to look for the lesson and grow through the experience.

In time you will look forward to those bumps in the road and see they are blessings in disguise.

One of the realities of existence is this: if you don't get it right the first time, life will give you another chance to master it. And if you miss your next chance, that same challenge will again present itself to you. The process continues until you get it right. This inevitable cycle is a curse if you are running away from your problems, but a blessing if you are seeking to grow through them. In every challenge lies an opportunity.

Appreciate Each Day

It seems that many of us are too rushed to appreciate each day. We're busy going off to work, to school, to catch a plane... busy being busy. Years ago we had predictions of shorter work weeks and more leisure time. Now we're so caught up in speed, gotta have it overnight, and computers that need to respond in nanoseconds, we don't take the time to appreciate the basic goodness of life. And where are we rushing to? Destinations we never quite reach even though we continue rushing to them each day. We have become the proverbial dog chasing its tail.

Life is not a race, and if it were it would be a relay where we work with and support each other rather than compete. So begin each day by giving thanks and you will see you'll have more time to enjoy your playing.

Remember, what you give attention to grows. Rather than giving attention to what you don't have, start focusing on and being thankful for what you *do* have. Often we live our lives on automatic, taking each experience for granted. We are so focused on the material aspects of life that we lose sight of everything else.

Recently, I spoke with a friend whose wife had surgery. They were thankful that initial indications showed all of the cancer was removed. You can bet they now have a consciousness of gratitude.

Who or what in your life are you taking for granted? Are you thankful for your eyes, your legs, your thumbs, and your ears? Do you appreciate your family and friends?

Several years ago I had my thyroid removed. Weeks before the surgery, I gave thanks that all parties involved were very skilled at performing this type of operation and that I would be divinely protected at all times. For me, giving thanks is a sign of appreciation and gratitude that also brings about a deep sense of peace. Ideally, you should give thanks beforehand. Even though you expect the best outcome possible, giving thanks in advance prepares you to accept whatever happens. My prayer is simply, "Thanks, God, for this or something better."

Starting right now, be more conscious of all the good life has to offer and say *thank you*.

I do believe

it's important

to believe in

something greater

than you are.

Tap into the Power of the Universe

Each person in this world is a jewel in a crown of unequaled beauty. I believe our imagination is the source of our individuality, our capacity for glory, and our own peerless talents.

The same life force present in the trees and plants is in you. When you have done all you can, turn it over to the renewing force within and let that same force help you meet and overcome your daily challenges.

We are all pieces of a cosmic puzzle. When we are closed to the ideas and suggestions of others, we might just be turning away the missing piece to complete our latest life puzzle.

Your Dreams Can Change the World

You can use the creative power
of your mind
to confront and shape
your unique reality.
Believe that your vision is important;
this awareness will involve you
emotionally in your activities.
Develop the ability to love
and enjoy everything that you do;
see your projects and experiences
as an extension of yourself.
This total investment will account
for a large part of your success.

Let your imagination run rampant.
Once you have dreamed your final goal,
construct the mental pictures
of the steps you can take toward it.
Then go out with a heart
filled with passion
and actualize what you have seen.

This technique is called
"the power of visualization,"
and it has been proven effective
by many successful people.

When you have faith in the outcome,
no matter what it may be,
you cannot stop yourself
from living and working
with enthusiasm.
As you put what you feel into action,
you are filled with vitality and happiness.
When you start out
with an attitude like that,
it enriches your life
and mobilizes the people
around you.

When you act according to
your highest dreams,
the outcome is often
far grander than you might imagine.

Don't wait by the roadside

for **success** to come along

like a crosstown bus.

Go out and **find** it, flag it down,

and **jump** aboard.

Make Success Your Destination

There is an anonymous poem
entitled "The Road to Success,"
in which the author writes that
the road to success is not straight.
One curve leads to failure,
another leads to confusion.
Friends and relatives
are the speed bumps
and flashing yellow caution lights
along the way.
Sometimes your job will seem
like a flat tire.
To get back on the road
and reach your destination,
you'll need a spare tire
called *determination*,
an engine called *perseverance*,
and an insurance policy called *faith*.
The bumpy road you travel
will feel smoother if you pack
a *positive attitude*
to bolster your belief in yourself,
plus plenty of *enthusiasm*
for whatever lies ahead.

What Is Your Life's Calling?

One of the first questions someone asks when they first meet you is "What do you do?" It's understood to mean "What do you do for a living?" or "How do you earn money?" When you think about it, if this country weren't so shackled by eighteenth-century Puritan values and repressive work ethics, we would ask "What do you do?" and we would mean "What do you do for fun?" or "What do you do to enjoy life?" or "What do you do to make people laugh, to make the world a better place, to spread love around the planet?"

Children barely able to stand on their two little feet are asked "What do you want to be?" As soon as they can speak, they are programmed to say they want to be a doctor, lawyer, firefighter, or maybe even stockbroker. In response to the question "What do you want to be?" they could instead be tutored to say, "I want to be happy," or "I want to be positive," or "I want to be well-adjusted, creative, filled with imagination, generous, grateful, helpful, and full of faith," or "I want to be in awe of the universe."

Your job, what you do for money, is not the same as you. Your source of financial security is not necessarily the source of your inner security. Some people stay at one job for twenty or thirty years or more. It's easy to admire them for the dedication and "stick-to-itiveness" — if their work fulfills them, rewards them, challenges them, makes them feel good, or makes their community or world a better place. Clinging to a meaningless job for the sheer security of having one is a different story.

If you can't find satisfaction and enjoyment in what you're doing, what's the sense of doing it? If you don't enjoy how you make your money, find another way. The reward is in the doing and being. You can always find another way, legally, to make money. And no matter what you do for a living, you can contribute to the betterment of our society simply by inspiring someone else.

Ask yourself... What is my destiny? What is my cause? What is my calling? If you could choose a title for what you want to be in this life, what would it be?

There is always

a *return* on the

love and *goodwill*

you offer to the world,

even though it often comes

back from people other than

those you *gave* it to.

Give Your Best to Yourself and the World

I am convinced that loving what you do plays a major role in your success. To be in love with your work means you would enjoy it even if you were not paid. The compensation is in the doing. In an age of cynics and people speeding to get nowhere, take time to reflect on how much you love what you're doing. If you find yourself lacking, look for ways to turn up your love.

Give your best to the world, because you have to live here until you leave. You are not a mediocre person; why not be the very best you can be? Bring forth the best in everything you touch and everyone you meet, and you, in turn, will become better and better. Everyone's life will be constantly enriched from without and within; the world will be better because you are here. Letting your enthusiasm burst forth is like letting your light shine. Don't live your life hiding under a basket. Let your enthusiasm be the beacon that brightens your day and enriches your life as well as the lives of others.

Develop a Positive Mindset

A positive attitude emphasizes perseverance over a challenge that may seem insurmountable. A positive attitude places more importance on the means than on the ends. A positive attitude also focuses on the solution and not on the problem. If you go through the day doing your best, at day's end you will look back and marvel at all you've accomplished.

Motivate yourself toward your goal constantly, even when you appear to be failing. Total commitment to your cause is like throwing a pebble into a lake; it creates ripples of value and good fortune throughout your life. Worthy results inevitably follow.

Your Potential Is Unlimited

Consider for a moment all the great thinkers and scientists; the great poets, playwrights, painters, and statesmen; the accomplished builders, business tycoons, athletes, and astronauts. They were born as humans; they ended or will end their lives as humans. They have all been pretty much the same inside as you.

Instead of putting yourself down, take stock of who you really are and what your capabilities are. Begin with a thorough self-examination. Enumerate your best assets, your God-given talents. You'll find that you have a lot to work with.

When it comes to being you, nobody does it better. You're the best you there is. You are the only you there will ever be. Remember, you choose how you see yourself. When you decide to accept your own self-worth, you embark on a life of peace, fulfillment, and achievement. And once you're happy with yourself, you can expect others to find qualities they admire in you.

Think of yourself as an *innovator* in your own life. You are a human being with as much human *potential* as your neighbor, your supervisor, or your president.

The Greatest Person in Your Life... Is You

Give to yourself enthusiastically.
Treat yourself with generosity.
Forgive yourself completely.
Balance yourself harmoniously.
Trust yourself confidently
    and completely.
You know what's right
and what's best for you.
Listen to your own small inner voice;
    don't ignore its urgings.
Above all, love yourself wholeheartedly...

Just remember, you're working
to improve you.
And what person in your life
is worth working on more?
Take good care of yourself.
You're important to the entire world,
but more importantly...
you are important to YOU.

About Wally Amos

Today, his name is a household word. Wally's most recent venture is Chip and Cookie, LLC, a retail store in Hawaii and online at www.chipandcookie.com, a business featuring two chocolate-chip cookie plush character dolls, Chip & Cookie, created by Christine Harris-Amos. In 1992, he formed Uncle Wally's Muffin Company, which produces a full line of muffins. As founder of Famous Amos Cookies in 1975 and the father of the gourmet chocolate-chip cookie industry, he has used his fame to support many educational causes. Wally was National Spokesman for Literacy Volunteers of America from 1979 until 2002, when they merged with Laubach Literacy Council to create ProLiteracy Worldwide. He now refers to himself as a literacy advocate whose primary focus is creating awareness of the values and benefits of reading aloud to children. He is also a board member of the National Center for Family Literacy and Communities in Schools.

Wally Amos has been the recipient of many honors and awards. He gave the shirt off his back and his battered Panama hat to the Smithsonian Institution's Warshaw Collection of Business Americana. He has been inducted into the Babson College Academy of Distinguished Entrepreneurs, and has received the Horatio Alger Award, The President's Award for Entrepreneurial Excellence, and The National Literacy Leadership Award.

In addition to this book, Wally has authored many other books, including his autobiography, *The Famous Amos Story: The Face That Launched a Thousand Chips, The Power of Self-Esteem,* and *Live an Inspiring Life.*

Over the years, Wally Amos has acted in a number of network sitcoms and appeared on hundreds of interview shows, news programs, educational programs, and commercials. On the lecture circuit, he addresses audiences at corporations, industry associations, and universities with his inspiring "do it" philosophy. His fame is grounded in quality, substance, and a positive attitude.